DUBAI, ABU DHABI

& The 5 Other Emirates You Didn't Know About

Diary of a Traveling Black Woman: A Guide to International Travel

Mini Travel Guide Series:

Teach Abroad: From Abu Dhabi to Abuja...

Jamaica: Likkle, but Tallawah!

Studying Abroad for Black Women

Iceland: Nature, Nurture, & Adventure

Solo Travel: Try It At Least Once!

And more...

Diary of a Traveling Black Woman:
A Guide to International Travel

"Mini Travel Guide Series"
Volume I - Dubai
3rd Edition

Dubai, Abu Dhabi
& The 5 Other Emirates You Didn't Know
About...

Nadine C. Duncan

The Traveling Black Women Network
Grace Royal International, LLC
Atlanta, GA

Cover Model: Nadine C. Duncan
Cover Design: Nadine C. Duncan
Interior Design: Nadine C. Duncan

ISBN: 9798986268064
ISBN: 9798986268071 (eBook)

Travel Guide Series, Volume I (3rd Edition)

Published in the United States by:
The Traveling Black Women Network
Grace Royal International, LLC
Atlanta, GA 30316

www.travelingblackwomen.com

For Dee Wilson
My First Friend in the UAE
The most genuine person I've ever known.

Contents

What to Know

Dubai is not a country!

Dubai is one of seven emirates that make up The United Arab Emirates (UAE). The other six emirates are Abu Dhabi—the nation's capital, Sharjah, Ras Al Khaimah, Umm Al Qaiwain, Fujairah, and Ajman. Founded in December of 1971, the UAE is a relatively young country that is growing and developing rapidly. Chances are, if you visit any part of the country again after a year or two of your first visit, you will have a totally different experience.

The UAE is located on the Arabian peninsula. Their government is described as a federation of monarchies. This means that the country is not a democratic state where the power lies with the people (as in the US). Instead, the UAE is an authoritarian state where the country's power lies with its rulers.

The UAE is bordered by Qatar, Saudi Arabia, and Oman. It sits directly across the Arabian Gulf from Iran and is a member of the Gulf Cooperation Council (GCC)—an alliance of wealthy Middle Eastern Countries that border the Arabian Gulf. This alliance includes Bahrain, Kuwait, Qatar, Oman, and Saudi Arabia. Depending on the airline you are traveling with, you are likely to have a layover in one of these countries. If you have a lengthy lay over during the day, I recommend leaving the airport and exploring. Many of the same rules listed in this guide apply to those neighboring countries.

As a young country, the United Arab Emirates has a steadily increasing population of over 10 million. Of that number, only about one-third of those individuals are actually Emiratis. The remaining population is made up of expatriates (expats) who have migrated to the new country for employment opportunities (including me).

DXB/AUH

The two major airports to consider when flying into the UAE for vacation is **Dubai Airport (DXB)** or **Abu Dhabi Airport (AUH)**. These airports are about 2 hours apart.

Currently, US Citizens only need a valid passport to travel to the UAE. Tourist visas can be obtained upon arrival. A few other countries, however, do require visitors to obtain their tourist visas in advance. Be sure to check the visa status before going because the requirements can always change.

Customs in Dubai – October 2022

Both DXB and AUH can be inconsistent with how their rules are enforced, so always err on the side of caution. Back in October 2022, my friend was stopped because she looked different in person than she did in her passport and in her visa photos. They held her for nearly an hour asking for additional verification of her identity. They even asked other agents for a second opinion on matching her identity to her passport.

Eventually, she was able to explain to them that she was simply wearing a different hairstyle in each photo and they let her enter the country. This situation was a perfect example of the nuances of traveling as a Black Woman. I would not have ever considered that the ever-changing hairstyles of Black Women could have been the deciding factor of my friend entering Dubai.

Getting Around

Car Rental

Renting a car is relatively easy and can be done at the airport when you land. You can use Google Maps or Waze to navigate Dubai and Abu Dhabi easily. If you plan to travel between Emirates or plan to be in the UAE for a long period of time you should definitely consider renting a car.

Be sure to familiarize yourself with the toll policy of the company you are renting from so that there aren't any surprises at the end. I'd also recommend using a credit card that will offer additional car rental coverage.

Driving Tips:
- Emiratis drive on the right-hand side of the road.
- The lane to the far left is the fast lane. You will be flashed or ran up on if you are driving too slow.
- Road rage exists, but as a woman... Don't get caught up. It is not worth it. A

verbal altercation or flipping someone off can have you locked up abroad.

- **Watch out for the speed cameras!** They are everywhere. Once your photo is taken, a ticket will be sent to the rental company.
- **Driving during Ramadan** - Do not eat or drink in your car during the daytime. You can actually be pulled over. As a Muslim country, the expectation during this time is that everyone is or appears to be fasting.
- **Roundabouts** - You will find that there are not many traffic lights in the UAE. Instead, you will see roundabouts to control traffic at intersections.

Taxis

Although renting a car is convenient, **Taxis** are extremely easy to find in well-populated areas. The traffic in some areas of Dubai definitely gives NYC vibes. Grabbing a cab in busy areas can be a hassle, but it's so much better than figuring out parking. More importantly it's safe, easy, and reliable. Careem, the UAE's ride-share app, also allows you to get picked up from your exact location by Taxi or registered vehicle. Women only Taxis with female drivers are also available and easily booked through the Careem app. All drivers are vetted and registered.

Public Transportation

Public Transportation is available throughout the UAE, however Dubai has the most access to multiple modes of public transportation that are clean, safe, and reliable. All public transportation include a Women's Only section and is easily accessible from Dubai's Main Tourist Attractions. Dubai's public transportation options include:

- **Dubai Bus**
- **Dubai Metro**
- **Dubai Tram**
- **Dubai Ferry**
- **Dubai Water Taxi**
- **Dubai Water Bus**

Abu Dhabi and the other Emirates still rely largely on their bus service (2023). I must point out that the UAE is a rapidly growing country, so I expect the other Emirates to have the same transportation access as Dubai soon. In the meantime, be sure to download the **nol app** for all your public transportation needs.

Language

Arabic is the national language of the UAE. Emiratis have their own Arabic "drawl" and slang. I would compare it to British English and American English where some words are clearly the same, while others are like... whaaat?

Nonetheless, connecting with the locals and other expats is fairly easy. Most people in the UAE speak English. Cab drivers, cashiers, waitresses, etc. are usually all expats from the Philippines, Ethiopia, and a myriad of other Southeast Asian and African countries. As a result, you may actually find yourself interacting in English with other expats more than the locals.

FYI-- Emiratis typically hold high ranking jobs that you would seldom need to interact with unless you are moving there or doing business.

Here are a few Arabic phrases to know:

- **Marhaba**—Hello; Welcome
- **Ma'Salama**— Good Bye
- **As Salaam A'laikum**—Peace be upon you.
- **Wa A'laikum Salaam**—And Peace be upon you too
- **Masha Allah**—God made her/him/it beautiful - "Wow"
- **Mafi Mushkela** (Mah'fi Moosh'keela)— No Problem; It's Ok!
- **Shu?** - What? / **Shu'Hatha**— What's this?
- **Shway Shway**—Little by little; Slow down; Excuse Me
- **Khalas (Kah'lahs)**—It's a Wrap/Stop!
- **Shukran (Shoo krahn)**—Thank you
- **Afwan (Aff'wahn)**—You're welcome
- **Hammam (Ha'mahm)**– Bathroom
- **Habibi**—My love (Term of Endearment)
- **Kham**—How much?

Numbers

1. Wa'hid
2. Ith'naan
3. Talatha
4. Ar'ba
5. Khamsa
6. Sit'ta
7. Se'bah
8. The'maan'ya
9. Ti'sa
10. Ashara

Colors

- As'wad—Black
- Ab'yad-White
- Ah'meer—Red
- Az'raq-Blue
- Ak'dar—Green
- As'far-Yellow

First Day of Work – September 2010

My first day of work in the UAE was the day I learned the phrase, "Al-Humdullilah." My first assignment in Abu Dhabi was at a Kindergarten school in a small region called Baniyas. After I received my assignment, I had no idea how to get to my school with the information that I was given nor I had not met anyone else who was at the same school that I could carpool or figure out the route with. I was told that most cab drivers knew landmarks pretty well and all I would need to do is name the school and the city and they would figure it out. Welp, they lied.

I hopped in a cab alone and rode out to Baniyas from Abu Dhabi City. It was wild to me that I was heading to my first day of work at a new school, in a new country, and riding down a highway lined with sand dunes and small herds of camel. It was surreal at the time.

When we arrived to Baniyas, my driver got completely lost. He took me to the wrong school and was hoping to drop me off and pull off. When I explained that we were at the wrong school before getting out, we resolved that he would take me to a local cab for the area and I could switch over to that cab service to navigate the area better. At that time, the Taxi system outside of downtown Abu Dhabi was still made up of locals in small cabs without meters.

When we found a local cab, we stopped and the drivers spoke to each other in Arabic. I paid the driver of the Abu Dhabi city cab and hopped into the Baniyas cab. I showed him the name of the school I was assigned to and naively assumed he spoke English when he answered, "OK!"

A few minutes later, I was at the wrong school again. At this point, I started to panic. I had no idea where I was or who I could call for help. I tried to speak to the driver and we could not understand each other at all. All he knew was, I was a teacher and it was my first day.

We drove to a few more schools, each of them wrong... and guess what? Ya girl started crying. I did not know what to do. I was scared. Who told my B*A* to move out here where I didn't know the language or the layout?? What was I thinking? And now, I was so deep into Baniyas, I didn't even know how to get home. Every news story of the Middle East starting playing in my mind.

Fortunately, my driver was patient. He noticed that I was starting to unravel. He kept saying "OK OK" to me and then words in Arabic that I didn't understand.

As we were driving around aimlessly, we saw a woman walking with her baby. He pulled alongside her and spoke to her in Arabic. She looked at me in the backseat looking pitiful and got in the car with the baby.

I didn't know what to think! She looked at me and asked if I was a teacher. Yes! I replied and showed her the information for my school. "KG OK" she said and then spoke to the driver in Arabic.

She stayed in the car with me while

the driver pulled off. Minutes later, I pulled up at the right school… two hours late, eyes red, and looking crazy. I thanked her repeatedly saying "Thank You! Shukran! Thank you!" while she and the driver smiled and responded "Al-Humdulilah! Al Humdulilah!"

I asked her to ask the driver how much I owed. He charged me around 150 AED which was about $40 USD. It was a little high, but considering the ordeal it took to get me there, I had no problem paying. The woman stayed in the taxi with her baby and I assume he drove her back home.

I walked into the school building and was greeted with "NADINE! AL HUMDULILAH!" They were waiting for me to arrive and were worried that I was lost. It was at that moment I recognized that there was a genuine concern for my safety regardless of the language barriers. I immediately felt at ease, got myself together, and started my first day of work. Al Humdulilah (Praise God)!

Sharia Laws

While Dubai and Abu Dhabi cater to Westernized tourists, those tourists are still expected be respectful of the laws that guide their religion and culture. These laws are known as Sharia Laws.

Sharia Laws dictate what behavior is considered illegal based on Islamic values. You can be imprisoned and deported for violations in the UAE whether you are aware of them or not. The key is simply to remember that you are a guest in their country. They will cater your needs as a guest/foreigner, but you are still expected to show mutual respect.

Here is a list of some things to keep in mind when traveling to the UAE. While the following list is not exhaustive, it is important to note that many of these acts are things we often take for granted. Therefore, it is important to be mindful of these expectations as you travel to this region.

Alcohol

Drinking alcohol is prohibited. Public drunkenness or drunk driving can land you in jail. **Restaurants primarily connected to hotels in high tourist areas serve alcohol.** If you want to purchase a bottle of alcohol, I recommend buying it at duty-free before leaving the airport. There are unmarked liquor stores sprinkled throughout the Emirates, but you will need to have a liquor license in order to purchase alcohol. (They may not always ask, but it's still good to have one just in case.)

Clothing

The UAE is not quite the place to let it all hang out! Even non-Muslim women are expected to be relatively conservative. While it may be hot, be careful with the booty shorts, tank tops, and see through clothing. Think cute, loose, and comfortable maxi dresses, linens, rompers, etc.

Dubai is the most relaxed of all the Emirates, but if you decide to venture into the other Emirates, including Abu Dhabi you'll notice that it is much more conservative. I'd recommend always taking a sweater or jacket with you. Now, I recognize that as Dubai gets more popular, it may appear that certain clothing is now acceptable. It's still not. Be aware of what is appropriate to wear and where.

Drugs

Drug laws are strict, including certain prescription drugs. Be sure to bring the appropriate documentation for any prescriptions you have. You can be promptly jailed and deported for possessing any illegal drugs or questionable prescriptions. Do not chance bringing drugs into the country.

Photography

Taking photographs of Emirati women without permission or in any "no photo" zone is illegal. You can be arrested or cited if caught.

PDAs

Sex between unmarried couples, homosexuality, kissing, holding hands (even if you are married), etc. is not allowed in most public establishments. I'd say anything that makes it obvious that you are boo'd up can be frowned upon.

Pork

Pork and all products using pork gelatin are prohibited. There are some hotels that serve pork and some grocery chains that have a private area where pork and pork products are sold for non-Muslims. Whenever you see bacon on the menu, it is most likely beef.

Ramadan

Eating, drinking, or chewing gum in public during Ramadan is forbidden. You can be cited for this offense; even in your own car.

Religious Activity

Although there are Christian churches in the UAE that are widely attended by expats, distributing religious, non-Islamic materials is illegal.

OK, but the reality...

This does not mean that you are not allowed to visit Dubai if you identify as LGBTQ+ or traveling with a significant other! Nor does it mean you can not drink, go to the club (which there are plenty of), or hug a friend in public. It simply means that you must be mindful of your surroundings at all times. Time and place is everything. It's also important to keep in mind that the UAE is a patriarchal society, which in my opinion means—the woman is always wrong, so be mindful of disclosing too much. Though the country is getting more lenient with tourists, don't get caught up on some foolishness.

What to Expect

The UAE's Black Community

You will see a lot of "familiar" faces while in the UAE. Since 2010, the Black community in the UAE has grown tremendously. This is due to the influx of professionals from around the world who have moved there to live and work.

What is most amazing about this community is that it is a mixture of the African Diaspora. You are sure to meet Black women from America, the UK, Africa, Canada, and the Caribbean.

This has also led to an increase in Black owned businesses throughout the Emirates that include beauty salons, Caribbean & African restaurants, fashion brands, event planning, and a host of other products and services. Check out pages like 'Black Girl in Dubai' to find out the latest before you go!

Notable
UAE Holidays

Despite what seems like a relatively strict society, Emiratis absolutely love to have a good time. Their cultural celebrations for weddings, National Day, Eid, etc. are truly exciting. Seeing Emiratis party and enjoy life is a reminder that even though laws like the Sharia laws seem restrictive, they only seem restrictive because they are unfamiliar to us as outsiders. It is important not to use our interpretation of those laws to assume that Emiratis, particularly Emirati women are unhappy with their way of life.

National Days

The UAE was formed on December 2, 1971. It can be compared to Independence Day, but it was not declared independent from any other country so the day is called "National Day." National Day celebrations take place on December 2 and 3 and is an all out celebration throughout the Emirate.

Emiratis are extremely patriotic! During this time you will see decorated buildings, highways, hotels, restaurants, homes, cars, etc. Everything seems to turn red, green, black and white overnight. At this time, Emiratis show the utmost respect for the country's Founding Fathers. You will the UAE flag and the photos of the Founding Fathers everywhere.

Ramadan

Ramadan is the holy month for fasting in the Islamic faith. During this time, Muslims abstain from eating, drinking, smoking, and sexual relations from sunrise to sunset. It is mandatory that tourists and expatriates of other religions are respectful of this time by refraining from eating, chewing gum (as it gives the appearance of eating), drinking, or smoking in public places. Many hotels and heavy touristy areas accommodate non-Muslims with covered or hidden areas in restaurants that still serve meals during the day.

You will also find that store hours will be altered to accommodate people who are more active after the sun sets. Some malls close as late as 1:00AM. Bars and lounges that remain open during Ramadan restrict their sales of alcohol to after sunset and do not play music at all.

Eid al – Fitr

Eid al-Fitr marks the end of Ramadan. Eid is a not only a religious holiday in the UAE, but it is also a National holiday. Schools & businesses close and the UAE throws a long weekend of celebrations. The city is decked out and the malls are full of sales.

Eid al – Adha

Eid al-Adha is another major Islamic holiday that is celebrated throughout the UAE as a National holiday. Expect schools & businesses to be closed and celebrations to be taking place everywhere!

*It is important to make note of the fact that while these holidays are considered religious holidays celebrated by a small group in countries like the US, it is a National holiday celebrated by ALL in countries like the UAE.

Climate

The UAE is HOT!!! I'm talking 90°F at dawn hot. I will say the heat is like nothing I've experienced before or since! When I first arrived in Abu Dhabi in 2010, I walked out of the airport and my glasses fogged up immediately! The heat engulfed me as if I had just stepped into a sauna. Within 45 seconds, I was sweating as if I was running a 5K. I was NOT ready.

Needless to say, there are only two seasons, hot and very hot. October to April is the "winter" season. Rain is unlikely. However when it does rain, it usually rains during this season. Temperatures, particularly out in the desert, can dip as low as 50°F at night and increase to about 90°F during the day. This is truly the best time to visit the UAE as the more bearable temperatures make it easy to explore the outdoors. Outdoor tourist attractions like Global

Village and Dubai Miracle Garden open during this season as well.

The summer months—May to September—are a different story. Luckily everywhere has the air conditioner blasting, so you may actually end up being cold more often than hot.

Temperatures during this time can range from a sweltering 90°F to 115°F daily. It is important that you stay hydrated in this heat as well as apply sunblock to your face. When I first moved to the UAE, I thought my melanin could handle a little sun. Little did I know, my Americanized melanin had become used to the Atlanta sun and wanted no parts of what the UAE had to offer. Within the first week, my cheeks began to break out like my skin was boiling. Almost as soon as I started applying facial sunblock with 50+ SPF, it cleared right up.

You will find that as a consequence

of this weather, Emiratis do more of their shopping, hanging out, etc. in the evening and at night. Places generally close pretty late. You can expect to see families with small children out and about at 11:00PM.

Despite the heat, conservative dress is still expected. Again, I'd recommend loose breezy clothing, linen, or long maxi dresses to keep you cool, cute, and out of trouble. As previously mentioned, the AC in most establishments is often very high, so it's always a good idea to keep a sweater, scarf, or jacket with you. After a while of being in the UAE, you will begin to see what places you can "feel free" to wear what you want in and what places you need to be more conservative.

Money

Currency in the UAE is called United Arab Emirates Dirham (AED). It is most often referred to as Dirhams. Currently (2023), $1.00 USD is equivalent to 3.67 AED.

All banks and establishments can easily access US funds. I personally have never had a problem using my American Visa or MasterCard at the ATM or in restaurants.

If you are going to the UAE to work, your employer will set up a local account for you. There are a number of currency exchange places that allow you to transfer money to your US accounts if necessary. If you are simply visiting, my recommendation would be to find the first Emirates National Bank of Dubai (ENBD) or National Bank of Abu Dhabi (NBAD) when you arrive at the airport and withdraw some spending money as opposed to using a currency exchange service. You will probably find yourself using your card most of the time anyway.

Before you go, download a currency converter app so you can keep track of your spending and nominal item costs. The UAE in general is not a very expensive to be, but it has a lot of high priced items and stores that give that impression. I felt the average spending to be in the range of spending a day in Downtown Atlanta or Time Square NYC.

Power

Power supply in the UAE is very different from the US. The voltage is somewhere between 220-240 and the plug is visually different. I've only witnessed problems with hair dryers and curling irons. Other than that, charging your phone or using your regular travel adapter should be fine.

Connect

The UAE has great Wi-Fi nearly everywhere, so connecting online to keep in touch or just post pics to make yourfriends jealous won't be a problem.

I'd recommend bringing an unlocked phone that you can slide a sim card into when you arrive. Etisalat and Du usually have a stand in the airport that will allow you to purchase a sim card when you land. The sales person will even set it all up for you. Having a sim card with data will make it easier to communicate and stay connected— especially if you plan on staying for a while. You can also use apps like WhatsApp or Google Voice to text or make and receive calls using voice over data. Trust me, it's better than giving US based companies all of your coins to stay connected.

What to Do

Here are just a few suggestions of what you can do in Dubai. This information only scratches the surface because Dubai and the UAE as a whole are rapidly changing. Reach out in the **Traveling Black Women Facebook group** and ask others for an update on what to do and where to go.

Restaurants

As a tourist, you'll notice that there are plenty of familiar restaurants in Dubai and throughout the UAE. You'll also notice that there are different cuisines from around the world readily available. Ironically, I found that it was difficult to find good local food in the midst of large chain restaurants and international cuisines. Be sure to check for updates before you go!

Accommodations

Luxury is common in the UAE. Mediocre is blasphemy. The standard of hospitality in the UAE is incomparable to anywhere else I've visited in the world. You really can not go wrong with where you choose to stay. Everything is big, bold, beautiful and well-maintained. As long as you demonstrate mutual respect, you will find that service workers will cater to your needs without pause. The only thing you really need to consider is what attractions you want to stay closest to and your personal favorite hotel brand.

I would recommend looking into hotel apartments and local hotel chains like *The Rotana*. I particularly like staying in hotel apartments because you get the comfort and amenities of a staying in full apartment (kitchen, washer & dryer, multiple bedrooms *and* multiple bathrooms) with front desk service at an affordable rate.

Dubai

The UAE prides itself on having the "only" or the "largest" (Fill in the Blank) in the world! Expect to be amazed by the size and glamour of a number of places.

Emiratis also love to eat and shop. Trust me when I say, you can land in Dubai with barely a toothbrush and be absolutely fine. Malls and shopping centers at every price point are everywhere!

Dubai Mall—Yes, the largest mall in the world. This is where a lot of major attractions, including the Dubai Aquarium, are located. They also have an ice skating rink, a million and one stores, and another million and one restaurants. No matter where you are from, you are guaranteed to see a store from your home country. I lived in the UAE for three and a half years and I still can't say I've seen that entire mall. I get tired just looking around

Burj Khalifa—SO, of course the largest mall in the world is adjacent to the tallest building in the world, the Burj Khalifa. The Burj Khalifa is a staple of the Dubai Skyline. It stands at 2,722 feet tall with 163 floors. This building breaks a number of world records. It even has one of the most beautiful NYE fireworks displays in the world. You can purchase a ticket to the top from inside the Dubai Mall.

Dubai Fountains—Right alongside the Dubai mall and the Burj is a courtyard with more restaurants, and an exotic pool of dancing fountains. The show is free but the area can get very crowded. The dancing fountains in Vegas do not compare. A few of the restaurants in the mall offer a great view!

Mall of the Emirates—This is where the indoor Ski Lodge known as Ski Dubai is located! Here you will find another myriad of familiar stores and restaurants. It is a gorgeous mall!

Burj Al Arab—Another exotic building that is a major landmark in Dubai. The Burj Al Arab is actually a hotel with average prices of over $1K a night! All restaurants require a reservation to visit. I spent 3.5 Years in the UAE and I've never been inside!

Dhow Cruise—This is Dubai's dinner cruise with a local feel. If you want a local food experience, along with sailing in a Dhow boat, I would definitely recommend it.

Desert Safari—This is most likely where you've seen your friends take pictures while jumping on sand dunes.

There are alot of companies to select from for Desert Safaris. You can find a good deal on Viator. Depending on what you choose, you'll get to ride a camel, watch the sunset (which is amazingly beautiful over the sand dunes), eat local food Beduoin style, ride ATVs in the sand, smoke shisha, and more...

Dubai Miracle Garden—This flower garden has millions of flowers molded into a variety of shapes and structures. It is an outdoor park so it is only open during the winter months. Opening and closing dates are announced each year on their website. This site is also another one of Dubai's superlatives: *The largest vertical garden in the world*.

Jumeirah Beach—Don't expect huge waves at this man made beach—just a spot to chill and look modestly good with a gorgeous view of the Dubai Eye.

The Walk @ JBR—In two words, this is "the strip." The Walk @ Jumeirah Beach is an area of restaurants and shops along Jumeirah Beach. It is perfect for strolling, people watching, and chillin'. This is where you'll see locals rolling through in fancy cars.

Palm Jumeirah— This gorgeous man-made island is amazing to see! The best view is from the air (helicopter or sky diving).

Sky Dive Dubai—If you are brave enough, you have to check out Sky Dive Dubai. I did it for my 29th birthday and it is still one of my greatest experiences abroad. You'll get the best view of the man made islands of Jumeirah.

Dinner in the Sky Dubai—I returned to Dubai in 2022 for my 39th Birthday and tried this amazing experience. Dinner suspended in the air? I'll try it! It is located right next to Sky Dive Dubai! The food wasn't the best but the views were spectacular.

Souk Madinat Jumeirah— The local markets are usually referred to as "The Souk." This particular Souk is a bit touristy, but you can find more in Bur Dubai and Deira. This is where you can get eclectic souvenirs and a gorgeous abaya (local dress for women) to take home.

The Old Souk— The old souk is located in Deira Dubai. Here you will find an outdoor market selling spices, gold at market prices, scarves, souvenirs, etc. I have to warn you, the salesmen are very aggressive here. This is the only place in the UAE that you will experience an aggressive market atmosphere where one "no" is not enough. Be prepared.

Global Village— Yes, more shopping. A huge global market with food and goods from around the world! It is usually only open from November—April, but it is certainly a place you want to visit and spend a couple hours shopping for souvenirs.

Waterparks— Considering the weather, I was not surprised when I realized the UAE had a number of waterparks! I can proudly say that I've been to every waterpark in the UAE built before 2013, even the one out in Ras Al Khaimah. If you are a waterpark lover, you have to make a trip to Aquaventure, Wild Wadi, or my personal favorite, Yas Waterworld.

Friday/Saturday Brunch— This is a must! Fridays in the UAE are like Sundays in the US. The locals consider Fridays a day for prayer, rest and family time. For expats or tourists, however, it's brunch time! Friday Brunch in the UAE is the ultimate "thing to do." Nearly every 4 or 5-Star hotel hosts a spectacular Friday or Saturday brunch with seafood, steaks, salads, bottomless drinks, etc. There are so many good boozy brunches that there should be a whole other guide for it! My favorites have been at every Rotana, Fairmont, Left Bank, Emirates Palace, Shangri-La, Ce La Vie, and Yas Hotel.

Henna—Full sleeves of traditional Henna are very common on arms and feet, especially during holidays and celebrations. Stop in any beauty salon that offers henna to get an authentic henna design that will last about a week. You can also get Henna done at touristy spots like the Desert Safaris or the mall, but the quality is not as good as a local salon.

Abu Dhabi

If you are visiting Dubai, there are a couple of sights you must see in Abu Dhabi to completely round out your trip. I would suggest renting a car and making the 90-120 minute trek to Abu Dhabi from Dubai and spending a day or two in UAE's capital city. Abu Dhabi is a great option if you are interested in getting a taste of more Emirati culture.

Friday Brunch—Abu Dhabi has amazing Friday/Saturday brunches as well. And, if you haven't guessed by now, Western food is often easier to obtain that local food.

Yas Island— Yas Island falls directly in between Dubai and Abu Dhabi. This is where you will find Westernized restaurants, more 5-Star hotels, and an amazing Golf Club. Yas also has a number of major concerts, Yas Waterworld, Ferrari World, Yas Marina Circuit and more.

Ferrari World— This is another must see, especially if you are into Theme Parks. Here you can ride the fastest roller coaster in the world, Formula Rossa. I rode it three times back to back. Not a good idea… but tons of fun!

Sheik Zayed Grand Mosque– This gorgeous mosque is the top attraction in Abu Dhabi City. If you don't go to Abu Dhabi for anything else, you should at least have the Grand Mosque experience. Appropriate dress and covering your head is a must. They no longer loan Abayas to visitors, so it is important that you arrive wearing loose, modest clothing or you will be denied entry. My aunt wore a long flowy dress in 2022, but was denied because there was a face printed on the front. She was able to purchase an abaya to cover her dress from the mall attached. If you aren't in the position to purchase an outfit on the spot, make sure that your clothing follows the guidelines.

Emirates Palace—This palace is actually a hotel. It is absolutely gorgeous. At Christmas time, you can expect non-Muslim and Muslim tourists alike flocking there to see the most expensive Christmas tree in the world.

The Corniche— The Abu Dhabi Beach is also a gorgeous sight. A nice spot to chill on the beach and people watch or just go on a stroll. The Corniche also has a number of beach concerts throughout the year.

Masdar City— If you are a techie with big dreams for the future, you will love Masdar City. Here you will get to experience driverless cars and other cool futuristic inventions.

Heritage Village— If you'd like to learn more about the Emirati culture, a stop at Heritage Village will give you a taste of how the Bedouin in the UAE once lived and how their lifestyle has evolved over the years.

Al Ain is a suburban area in Abu Dhabi with even more sights.

Here are just a few:

Wadi Adventure– Wadi Adventure is an adventure park that has everything from surfing, wild water rafting, ziplining, kayaking, etc.

Camel Souk– You can walk around the Camel Pens for free or take a tour for a few dirhams.

Jebel Hafeet— This is the second highest peak in the Emirate with loads of history. It is definitely worth a quick stop!

The 5 Other Emirates

The 5 other Emirates that many tourists don't know about are:

Ajman

Fujairah

Ras Al-Khaimah

Sharjah

Umm al-Quwain

These emirates are more conservative than Dubai and Abu Dhabi, but rich with the true Emirati culture. I learned the most about UAE's cultural history while at work and when visiting these other Emirates.

Each Emirate is governed by its own ruler. Although you will still find alcohol being sold at the hotels, the expectations for modesty is much higher.

Ajman

This is the smallest Emirate. This Emirate is described as the most laid back with plenty of beaches, historical sites, and even their own **Sheikh Zayed Mosque.**

Fujairah

Musandam Dhow Cruise (Dibba) - If you have time to make it to Fujairah, the Dhow Cruise to Oman and back is absolutely gorgeous! You can book a tour that will pick you up from Dubai or Abu Dhabi and drive you out to Fujairah for the cruise. There is usually a lot of local food and time carved out to swim near the caves.

Ras Al– Khaimah

Jebel Jais (Ras Al Khaimah) - The highest peak in the UAE. If you are into scenic situations, a drive out to Ras Al Khaimah would be amazing.

Sharjah

Sharjah is a close runner up to Dubai & Abu Dhabi. **Al Majaz Waterfront & The Sharjah Eye** is a great spot for walking and just hanging out. Lots of local shopping (of course), and good restaurants.

Umm al–Quwain

Fort Al-Ali is a notable attraction in this Emirate for tourists that like history. It dates back to the mid-1700s when the emirate was ruled by the Al Mualla Royal Family.

Nightlife

Despite all the laws and general expectations for modesty, Dubai has an amazing nightlife. There are a number of bars, lounges, and nightclubs with amazing drinks and good music.

Nightclubs in Dubai are easy to locate because they are usually connected to hotels (remember the alcohol rules). I'd recommend connecting with expats before going so you can find out about parties, upcoming concerts, and other pop up events.

Make sure you research the music for the night that you want to go to a particular club as each night at most clubs have a different vibe. I'd recommend checking for an updated list of clubs by doing a search for the top 10 clubs that play your favorite music.

So…. That is Dubai, Abu Dhabi, and the rest of the UAE in a nutshell. It is truly a great place to visit, live, and work if you are culturally aware of the differences and prepared to respect them.

I must warn you, if briefly adapting to another culture's way of life feels too uncomfortable for you, I would not recommend going to Dubai.

If you read no other part of this book, make sure you go back and read the section about Sharia Laws. These laws govern how the UAE handles all incidents that take place in their country. It is important to recognize that once you leave the US, you also leave some of "your rights" behind.

I would recommend registering on the Smart Traveler Enrollment Program (https://step.state.gov) if you have any worries or concerns about traveling to Dubai or any where else in the United Arab Emirates.

...Diary...

Nadine C. Duncan

Diary of a Traveling Black Woman:
A Guide to International Travel

Dubai, Abu Dhabi & the 5 Other Emirates You
Didn't Know About...

Trinidad: More Than Just Carnival...

About the Author

Nadine C. Duncan, EdD is an educator with over 15 years of experience in P12 education. Her primary educational focus is serving special populations--special education, gifted, and ESL. She has taught at all grade levels as well as served as a job developer for post-secondary youth.

Nadine also spent time abroad serving as a Head of Faculty in the United Arab Emirates. Upon returning to the United States, she founded the Traveling Black Women Network and published several international travel guides to center the Black women's travel experience.

In 2018, she founded Grace Royal International and expanded her publishing company to include biographical fiction, poetry and other such genres under the imprint, A Divine Journey.

You can learn more at
www.nadinecduncan.com

www.travelingblackwomen.com

www.ingramcontent.com/pod-product-compliance
Lightning Source LLC
Chambersburg PA
CBHW040856120626
46551CB00001B/41